The
Family
and
Prayer

The *Family* and *Prayer*

...their impact
on
today's society

John Olsen, CFX
and
Thomas Masters (eds.)

New City Press

Published in the United States by New City Press
206 Skillman Avenue, Brooklyn, New York 11211
©1991 New City Press, New York

Cover design by Nick Cianfarani

Library of Congress Cataloging-in-Publication Data:

The family and prayer : . . .their impact on today's society /
  John Olsen and Thomas Master (eds.).
      p. m.
    ISBN 0-911782-94-X : $6.95
    1. Family—Religious Life. I. Olsen, John, CFX. II. Masters,
  Thomas.
    BV4526.2.P73 1991
  248.4—dc20   91-27205

Printed in the United States of America

Table of Contents

Part III
Commitment, Light and Joy

Introduction

Family life in the United States has been clearly weakened and fragmented during the last twenty-five years. The structure of family life has been altered by divorce, temporary commitment, delay in marriage, by reduction in size, by choices of careers with both parents working, and by single parent homes.

The writings of our recent popes, including Pope Paul VI, have called attention to the role of the family in transmitting Christian values and ideals. Council documents have stressed the primacy of the family in evangelization and in education. Pope John Paul II referred to the parents as the "first heralds of the gospel for their children."

The bishops of the United States have sought to make specific this primacy of the family. In a document entitled, *Sharing the Light of Faith: National Catechetical Directory for Catholics of the United States* (approved in the Vatican Congregation in October 1978), the elements for Catholic education in the home as well as in the school are specified and developed. It indicates that the home is the critical educational institution and challenges the parish to be "an intensive support system for family life." These elements focus on the Word of Life, the message of the gospel; on the unity of the family as community; on prayer and liturgy, particularly the rosary and the Mass; and on the outward expression of this unity, the service to the neighbor, however expressed. The *Directory* says "members of families need extensive support if they are to grow in faith and live according to the example of Christ and the teaching of his Church."

This is the focus of *The Family and Prayer*. The reader will find here not only viable principles and motivations but, more concretely, life-giving experiences of contemporary families from throughout the United States and of parents and children in them, who share the fruits of trying to live out their values and beliefs in their ordinary daily efforts.

The place of prayer and worship in the family is herein emphasized as part of this educational and communitarian life in the home. The *Directory* says "Individuals and communities also pray in word and ritual. Thus prayer helps people achieve and express the reality of internal self-surrender to God, which lives in the depths of consciousness and flows into life." The reader will find enrichment in the realities of families who pray together, thus finding ways of maintaining family unity.

Unity which nurtures love and mutual charity is at the heart of the Focolare movement whose spirituality of unity animates this book. *Focolare* means fireplace or hearth. It is a symbol of the home, of the warmth and fire which sustains and energizes the relationship of members of the family. The name was given to Chiara Lubich, the foundress, and to her early companions by those who witnessed the effects of mutual love and the sustained effort to live out the phrase of the gospel, "Where two or three are gathered in my name, there am I in their midst" (Mt 18:20).

The experiences contained in this book are introduced by the address of Chiara Lubich to the International Family Congress of 1990 which was held in Rome. The address was entitled "The Family and Prayer." The relationship of prayer to family life is seen to be at the heart of the role of the family in society.

The social implication of this message of family life centered on God is that exhortation of Vatican II: "While helping the world and receiving many benefits from it, the Church has a single intention: that God's kingdom may come, and that the salvation of the whole human race may come to pass."

The experiences which follow Chiara Lubich's address were presented at local sessions of the Family Congress throughout North America. They are real, they are vital. They do not attempt to provide simple solutions to complex

8

social problems but to offer signs of encouragement and of possibility in entering the painful struggle of growth in depth and in unity. They are an attempt to share light, the light of faith. They model aspects, sometimes painfully simple and ordinary, of a new life which is being born in the world today. They are an attempt by these families, in their own words and idioms, to share the light which has come into their lives, which makes every particular situation an opportunity to grow closer to one another, to their neighbors, and to God.

May you, the reader, find encouragement and support from this book, and may you apply in your own way and according to your own lights and gifts, the life and the ideals which are shared by the many authors of this work.

Part I

THE FAMILY CENTERED ON GOD

The Family and Prayer

by Chiara Lubich

Our congress, as you know, is entitled: *"Family and Society: the Family Centered on God is Open to all Humanity."*

Centered on God. In this part of our program today we will say something about the relationship that the family has, or should have with God, the Absolute—so it's a rather special theme. And since this relationship can be defined with one word, prayer, we will speak about *the family and prayer*. It is an important, urgent, demanding and decisive topic which can help the family to carry out its role in a truly effective way. So this talk is like a meditation.

However, to discuss this theme in depth, I think it will be helpful, considering today's society, to begin by looking briefly at the reality of the family. Likewise, it will be useful to reflect on the meaning that prayer generally has in the life of individuals. . . .

The family

The family! Today there is a head-on attack against the family, and the situation seems to be getting worse. The family is so threatened, if not ruined, by the decline of traditional moral values, by theoretical and practical materialism, by the hedonistic mentality favored by a consumer society, that many people are forced to question themselves: what meaning, what importance does the family have?

Sociologists, educators, politicians and moralists could offer their opinions. I believe that we Christians are interested above all in trying to understand God's idea of the family, and the importance he gives to it.

13

A few considerations will suffice to understand this. When God created the human race, he formed a family. When the Word of God came on earth, he willed to be born in a family. Jesus began his public life during the celebration of a new family.

God had the family so much at heart, he considered it to be of such importance that he impressed on it his own image. In fact, the family reflects God's very own life, the life of the Holy Trinity. This is sufficient to say what the family means to God.

What was God's plan for the family? God who is love, thought of the family as an intertwining of relationships of love: nuptial love between the couple, maternal and paternal love towards the children, filial love toward the parents, the love of grandparents for their grandchildren, of the grandchildren for their grandparents, for their uncles and aunts and vice versa. The family is therefore a repository, a jewel, a mystery of love.

This is how God thought of and created the family. And his Son, in redeeming the world, turned this natural love, with which the members of the family are impregnated, into something sublime through the divine love he brought on earth, through the fire that he wants to burn everywhere. Through him, the family has become not only the primary cell of humanity created by God, but also the basic cell of the Church founded by his Son.

Because of the supernatural love that the members of the family have for one another—through baptism and the other sacraments, particularly the sacrament of matrimony—they are called individually and collectively to the sublime heights of making the family a small church, an *ecclesiola*.

Prayer

And now, something on the meaning of prayer in general. What is prayer? Is prayer important? We might not believe it, or we may never have thought about it, but prayer is something essential to our very being.

14

This is true because we have been created in the image of God. This means that we have the possibility of putting ourselves in the presence of God, certainly, as creatures in front of our Creator, but also as the "you" of God. We are capable of establishing a relationship with God, of being in communion with him. This possibility is so typical of human beings that it constitutes our very being—it expresses who we really are. We are not truly ourselves if we do not fulfill this specific vocation.

But to grow in our relationship with God, to be in communion with him means to pray. Therefore, only if we pray are we fully as God planned us to be when he created us.

Our fundamental vocation to prayer becomes evident when we consider people of the most varied religions. Everyone feels inclined to turn toward God or toward a supreme being. In our contacts with brothers and sisters of other religious beliefs, we have discovered texts of prayers which are truly beautiful. They bear witness to the secret but effective action of God who urges people to pray.

Looking at our own experience, we can see that even in our times, in our de-christianized world, where the center of life is no longer God but human beings (or science, technology and progress), there is a return, a desire, a thirst for prayer, especially among young people. It is a sign that in every epoch our true nature emerges: our being in the image of God.

Is prayer only a personal concern? Prayer is basically a personal concern, but it would be a mistake, especially for us Christians, to consider it only in this way. We are united to one another in the mystical body of Christ. This is a mystery which we can understand to a certain extent by thinking of containers which are interconnected. When water is placed into one of the containers, the water level increases in all of them. The same thing happens when we pray. Prayer is the elevation of our soul to God, and when we are elevated to him, also the others are elevated. So although Christian prayer is a personal concern, it is also a communal, ecclesial reality.

15

This is true always, but it holds true especially for the various expressions of liturgical prayer, which is the apex of Christian prayer because it is the prayer of the Church itself.

I began by giving a few ideas on the family and on prayer so as to better understand both. Now let us look at prayer in the family, at the family's prayer.

Relationship between family and prayer

Is there a relationship between the family and prayer? Does the family have anything to do with prayer? Yes, certainly!

The primary reason for this is that prayer begins in the family. It *must* begin in the family. Families are the first schools of prayer. Right from their earliest years, children should begin to perceive a sense of God and worship him. In fact, what we learn as children, also in this field, remains for the rest of our lives. If prayer is not taught in the family, it will be difficult to fill this emptiness later on.

We know that what children learn during the first three years of their lives concerning the supernatural or the divine is essential. Therefore, it is necessary to look after them, especially during their first years and at least until they reach the age of six.

Thus the evangelization of the young, of the world's future, depends largely on the "domestic church," on the *ecclesiola*.

Parents: bearing witness to God

How can parents effectively carry out their task as teachers of prayer? So that children may learn to pray to God, it is necessary first of all to unveil to them the reality of God. They must discover his existence. They must know that he exists.

Parents have an extraordinary opportunity: they can instill this knowledge into their children by bearing witness to him.

"May they all be one," (in love and in truth) Jesus says in the gospel, "so that the world may believe" (Jn 17:21). May Christians love one another so that the light of faith may radiate in others.

If the often unbelieving world of adults, fossilized by materialism, secularism and other forms of evil, can be touched by the unity of Christ, by our reciprocal love, to the point of making them believe, all the more will the innocent, small world of our children be touched by this witness. It will make them understand that there is Someone who envelops us all with his love and they will spontaneously turn their minds and hearts to him with confidence.

Thus only fathers and mothers who daily live mutual and constant charity, who strengthen and consolidate their human love and transform it into supernatural love, can effectively enter the hearts of their children, leaving traces which future events in life will never be able to cancel.

However, mutual love must be put into practice in the right way, so that it responds perfectly to what Jesus commands. Jesus wants the husband to see and love in his wife, not only the person with whom he shares his life, but to see and love Christ himself in her. In fact, Jesus considers done to him whatever the husband does to his wife and vice versa.

Furthermore, Jesus in the husband or wife must be loved in the measure that Jesus requires, as he expressed with the words, "Love one another as I have loved you" (Jn 13:34). They must love one another to the point of being ready to give their lives for one another. If parents keep this in mind throughout the day, whether they are praying, working or eating, whether they are resting or studying, laughing or playing with their children . . . , every moment will be an opportunity for bearing witness to God.

Not only this, but through their testimony, which demands sacrifice, parents will be more convincing reference points for their children. Jesus said, "When I am lifted up from the earth, (and in some measure this applies

17

to Christians too) I will draw all people to myself" (Jn 12:32). They will become models for their children.

If parents pray together, also making use of external expressions like kneeling down, making the sign of the cross or reciting vocal prayers, the little ones will imitate them. They too will try to kneel down, to make some kind of sign of the cross. Perhaps even in their early years, they will stammer something without understanding anything, but simply led to do so by their parents' example. Then the time will come to teach them to pray orally. The short prayers that children learn are the beginning of their dialogue with God.

Then, as the years pass, children can learn more specific prayers. Parents should take this task to heart. We should remember the grief-stricken invitation of Paul VI to parents: "Mothers, do you teach your children Christian prayers? . . . And you, fathers, do you spend a few moments of prayer with your children, with the entire domestic community? Your example . . . supported by a few common prayers, is worth a lesson of life. It is worth an extraordinarily valuable act of worship" (general audience, August 11, 1976).

Thus prayer in the family is born and blossoms into a splendid habit.

Praying together united in the name of Jesus

Prayer in the family is a special prayer. It is not just like any other personal prayer. It is exceptionally effective. In fact, Jesus promises to those who pray together united in his name, his very own presence: "Where two or three," he affirms, "are gathered in my name, I am there in their midst" (Mt 18:20). He is there to pray with the family; in the family is Jesus himself, the almighty, who can do everything.

And if he is present, how can the Father not listen to him? The family will soon experience God's providence. Faith will grow and with it prayer will be given new value.

How and when to pray

In teaching us to pray, Jesus mentioned two things which may seem to be contradictory, but they are not. He affirmed, "When you pray do not use many words" (cf. Mt 6:7) and "pray always" (cf. Lk 21:36).

Every family should follow these two directives.

Do not use many words. When?

During the day there are precise moments in which the family is called to pray. And there are various prayers which Christian piety has taught and teaches for these circumstances. It is not possible to list them here. Perhaps it would be more useful to say what we feel is fundamental in each one.

What is fundamental in the different prayers

When we wake up in the morning, we immerse ourselves into the supernatural world we became part of through baptism, by saying brief prayers to our heavenly Father, to Jesus, to Mary. . . . This is the moment to offer God our entire day. We must love God and to love means to give, so we give him every new day.

Then during the day, involved as we are in worldly matters (work, study, recreation,) it is indispensable for the members of the Christian family, either together or individually, to find the courage to withdraw from the world around them and to devote a few minutes, "to seek," as St. Paul would say, "the things that are above" (Col 3:1).

It means that we think of the world of our faith and penetrate it. It means that we meditate, or as our young people say, that we go in-depth. It also means that we read some phrases from scripture, especially from the gospel, pausing to reflect on one point or another, which has struck us, and drawing useful resolutions for our life. What is fundamental in this kind of prayer is to seriously put ourselves in contact with God, as his children, in order to draw strength and light.

19

In the past, also the rosary was said in the family. And this is understandable because by doing so we are able to review the mysteries of our faith every day. We are able to praise Mary over and over again: "Hail Mary, full of grace . . . blessed are you among women." A person who feels just a little bit of love for Mary willingly says the rosary because a person who loves never grows tired of expressing words of love to the person he or she loves.

The Church still advises us to say the rosary. But if this seems to be too much for us, can we not recite a part of the rosary? Basically, this prayer develops our relationship with the person who, in God's plan, is the way, the gate that unites us to God, and hope, also because she is the mother of every Christian family.

In the evening, before going to bed, the family can say another brief prayer together, as in the morning. We can give thanks for our day and also make an act of contrition for the mistakes we made and resolve to do better the next day.

These are some of the prayers that can be said in the family throughout the day, and for those who can, there are many other wonderful initiatives, like going to Church to visit Jesus who is always too alone.

And on days which present different needs, the family has many opportunities to meet together and invoke God's help: for the success of an exam, for instance, for the birth of a child, for a sick person in the family, for a financial problem, for the solution to a spiritual crisis. Jesus said, "Ask and it will be given to you; seek and you will find; knock and it will be opened to you" (Mt 7:7). And if he said this, it is true.

The Mass

Then there is Mass which is the apex of all prayer. On Sunday, the Lord's day, the family, this small church, immerses itself in the Christian assembly which gathers together. The family listens to the word of God. It partakes in the bread and cup of Christ and then it extends its communion with the eucharist to fraternal communion.

Through the Mass the members of the family can feel that their hearts are satisfied; they can feel abundant peace.

In fact, we would always want to offer God something fitting to his majesty, something worthy of him. However, our offering is so out of proportion to his greatness that it is very consoling to know that in the Mass, together with the priest, we can offer Jesus himself to the Father. We can offer his sufferings which are of immense value and we can unite our sufferings to his, to adore the Father, to love him, to praise him, to glorify him worthily, to thank him, to ask him for graces and to ask him in a suitable way to forgive our mistakes.

Pray always, pray well

"Do not say many words," but Jesus also says, "Pray always and never lose heart" (Lk 18:1).

Pray always. How can we do this? And how can we do this especially in the vortex of our daily living? By making every action an act of love for him, possibly preceding every action, as we often do with the more important action, with the words, "For you," as some of the saints have taught.

"To pray always" does not mean that we should multiply our prayers, but that we should direct our hearts and our entire lives to God. We should study for him alone, work and exert every effort, suffer, rest and also die for him alone.

And we should carry out every action in the best way possible, because we know that we can make it an extension of God's creative action and the redemptive action of Jesus towards the achievement of God's plan for the world. Thus all our actions can be transformed into sacred actions.

And this way of praying is very much in tune with our times. Today we see the world and all the universe in evolution, and human beings are reminded of their duty to "subdue the earth" (cf. Gn 1:28). It is especially through this way of praying that we fulfill the command of Jesus: "Pray always" (cf. Lk 21:36).

Of course, it is also necessary to pray well. We should always begin with a few moments of recollection in order to realize that we are in front of God.

We should pronounce well the words suggested to us by the Church, in order to make them our own and to say them with all our heart.

We can also pray spontaneously, confiding to Jesus and Mary our innermost secrets. We can tell them how much we want to love them and how much help we need. We can tell them our difficulties, our hopes and plans.

We should pray with faith. "If you have faith and never doubt . . . even if you say to this mountain: be taken up and cast into the sea, it will be done" (Mt 21:21).

These are some ideas on prayer in the family. If it is not possible to do everything, which is probably the case, let us do at least something. If we cannot gather together to pray with all the members of the family, let us do so with those who are willing. In any case, there must be prayer in the family. The family as such, especially today, needs the protection of heaven.

Love of neighbor: way to union with God

I would like to add a consideration and a suggestion.

In our times, we are stimulated more than ever before by a thousand factors. We live in a world that offers continuous amusements, news and images. The television, radio, telephone and so much noise deafen us. Even without wanting it, even with a certain amount of control, we are all subjected more or less to the many sounds that reach our ears. We can hardly help receiving the many ideas supplied by the media. It is difficult to free ourselves from what we could honestly call a bombardment. It is more likely that we end up being dominated by these ideas, if not downright attracted by them.

How can we withdraw ourselves in order to devote some

time to prayer? Yes, of course, we can use our reason and good will strengthened by faith. But we can also follow the indications of the Holy Spirit, who never ceases to help people of every epoch. We can follow the suggestions he gives precisely for people of our times.

We live in an epoch in which the role of the laity is highlighted in the Church. The laity was the particular object of study during the recent Synod, and the Apostolic Exhortation *Christi Fideles Laici* noted how the Holy Spirit looks at the laity with special love, by enkindling, for example, movements with spiritualities suited to them.

In order to bring the laity to full union with God, these spiritualities do not remove them from their environments. They do not ask them to do hard penances or make prolonged fastings in order to guarantee an authentic Christian life, as might have happened in the past. Rather, they encourage the laity to find their way to God right there in the midst of the world, where they live shoulder to shoulder with neighbors of every kind.

These spiritualities emphasize that the heart of Christianity is love of neighbor out of love for Christ, because in this consists the fulfillment of the law. They teach and urge the laity to live this love and to restore it if it has been shattered because without this love not even one's offering to God is acceptable; to constantly put this love into practice, sharing with the people they meet in life their fatigues, anxieties, worries and joys.

These spiritualities invite the laity to make this love the reason of their lives. And this is the divine wonder: when these committed lay people, fully determined to love their neighbors throughout the day, forgetting about themselves, are recollected in prayer, they find God himself deep down in their hearts. God invites them to a profound union with him. They feel his love, and a spontaneous, loving conversation begins. This is a marvelous experience which everyone can make.

What takes place is similar to the life of a plant—the more its roots sink deep into the soil, the higher its stem rises up towards the sky. Here, the more we enter into the heart of our neighbor to share his or her sufferings and joys, the more our soul rises to union with God.

Conclusion

Are there forces and stimuli in today's society which strongly attract people towards the outside world, often made up of vanities that almost hypnotize people, that mortify their creativity—their thoughts, for instance—that imprison and deceive them by promising an easy happiness?

Well there is also an inner force in the depths of people's hearts which attracts them and immunizes them from the spirit of the world. It calls them to a special type of prayer and offers them a peace which the world does not know, joys which are incomparable with those of the world and consolations which fully satisfy them.

May the family, the small lay church, learn to walk along these new ways that the Holy Spirit is pointing to in our day in order to reach the Lord. May it learn to experience these sublime effects of love, through which every other prayer in the family acquires new depth. In this way, the family will belong to God always more and God will be able to accomplish his plan for the family. He will make it open to many other families so that all together they may form the vast family of the sons and daughters of God, who are linked by the love brought by Jesus and who bear witness to how the entire human family should be in the world.

May Our Lady, singular vessel of devotion (prayer), look at all our families. May she enwrap them with her maternal love. May she make them similar to her family, the holiest family that ever existed or will ever exist—the family with Jesus, her son, and Joseph, her husband.

Part II

Living the Reality of Family, the Experience

Chiara Lubich's address on prayer underlined that which stands at the heart of Christianity, love of neighbor for love of Christ. It is this thrust then that draws us closer to God and then when we turn to him in recollected prayer we find a profound and spontaneous dialogue that has in effect already been started.

The concrete and seemingly ordinary experiences which are presented here are models of real people putting the ideals we have just read about in Part I into practice. They inform and they stimulate us to put the principles of Christian family living into practice.

They are experiences that focus on the internal life and unity of the family itself and explore the various relationships that grow and develop among spouses, children, and grandparents. They represent, in a certain respect, normal everyday families that have accepted the challenge of being "centered on God and open to all humanity."

Praying Together

One of the most important things our family does each day is pray together. Even though we have ten children at home, ranging in age from four to twenty-two, who have different activities and different schedules, we still manage to come together in the morning, at dinner, and in the evening to pray. Many people over the years have asked us, "How do you get the children to pray with you?" We are not sure we know all the reasons, but we think we know some of them.

For one thing we start praying with our children from the time they are born so that praying together becomes an essential part of what we all do each day in our family life. Just as getting dressed, washing our faces, and brushing our teeth become normal routines each morning, so does praying with our family. Praying is thus not something unusual, something added on to regular life; it becomes a part of the normal rhythm of each day's activities.

Another thing that helps is to keep our prayers short. If they drag on too long, the little ones get restless and the teenagers get distracted. Our morning and evening prayers, for example, take only a few minutes. In the mornings, we recite the traditional prayers: the Morning Offering; Our Father; Hail Mary; Glory Be; and Angel of God. During the Mideast crisis and war we began a "Time Out" for peace. The "Time Out" is a prayer recited by thousands of people all over the world at the same time every day. It's a moment to just stop and pray together for world peace. In the evening we add prayers for those in need and for any family

27

member not present. We try to have dinner together each evening and say grace before we start; on special feasts, like Christmas and holy days, we like to sing a short but beautiful prayer that a friend of ours composed in three-part harmony.

We feel that it is very important to include the younger children in our prayer life. We noted how all of our children have gone through the stage of curiously observing us while we were praying together. At some point between the ages of one and two, they would stop and look around to see with whom we were talking. Little by little they learned that although they could not see him, God was present, for all the people they trusted most—their mother, father, brothers and sisters—were surely talking to someone. And since they were baptized and had the gift of faith themselves, it was not hard for them to believe too. They soon realized that their family was speaking to Someone who is great like a king (they kneel before him), and who they love very much (they call him "Father").

The power of this example is almost impossible to exaggerate. It is a much more effective teacher than all the explanations we could give our children about the existence and omnipresence of God, for it gives them a living experience of the reality of the supernatural. They "see" God as the most important and central part of their family life. God is the first one we give our attention to in the morning and the last one we think about at night.

A third thing we do—it is tiny but helpful—is to always invite the youngest child to begin our time for prayer. One of us parents will ask him or her, "Elizabeth, what are we doing now?" and we teach her to respond, "Talking to God." This is the signal that we all have to stop talking and whatever else we were doing and settle down—"recollect" ourselves, as was once commonly said. This not only gets little Elizabeth involved actively in the praying activity but calls all of us to make an act of faith and focus on God.

This third item sometimes—not too often though—gets extended a bit. After the youngest says, "Talking to God," we might then ask, "Who is God?" and then see what the youngest says first, until we get a brief definition like "The one who made us and all things." The next day or so, we might repeat this question and add another: "Why did God make you?" Usually they answer, "Because he loves us." Finally, we might ask, "How do you know God loves you right now?" Here the older children can't resist blurting out our favorite answer: "Because if God stopped loving us right now, we would disappear!" If they are used with discretion, these questions help not only the little ones but all of us focus more intently on what we are about to do and what prayer really means: speaking in response to a God who is present and who is loving us right now.

We also pray together as a family when crises come, like the death of a relative or the sickness of a friend. At these times we remind each other that Jesus promised "whatever you ask in my name, I will give you," and we begin our prayer in this way: "Eternal Father, in the name of Jesus, we ask you . . ." When I received a phone call that my father had just died, for example, I remember we were all in the kitchen and we immediately stood close together and asked the Father to bring him to heaven and we spoke with confidence because we asked all together and "in the name of Jesus."

A couple of years ago, we were shocked to find that we mistakenly took too many deductions on our income tax so that we had to pay $900 by April 15. Since in our large family we live on a very tight budget and since we expected to receive our usual tax refund, we were not at all prepared to pay so much money. We soon realized that we would have to rely on God's providence in this emergency. My wife suggested that we go to a nearby chapel and pray before Jesus in the eucharist. We had done this so many times before that we were at peace and very confident because we knew that God loved us. So we went like little children and asked our Eternal Father for $900 by April 15.

Within a week surprising things started happening. Although I never did any sort of outside consulting beyond my regular work—I never ever thought of such a thing—I was suddenly offered out of the blue a one-day job as a consultant for $250. A week or so later, my wife was able to teach a class on the weekend that brought in another $200. Then small amounts came trickling in from different sources that amounted to $150. By the beginning of April we reached $600. We were sure the last $300 would arrive on time.

The following week I got a letter from an old friend I had gone to college with. I hadn't seen him for a long time since he was working in another country. He wrote that he was thinking about us and for some reason he "felt that we could use some money right now." Enclosed in the envelope we found a check for $300.

Other fruits of our praying together are the changes that have taken place in our children. We have been trying for a long time to live the gospel in our family and we believe in the promise of Jesus: "Where two or three are gathered in my name, I am there in their midst." So we try to live in his name by working hard to do what he asked, "Love one another as I have loved you." We experience much peace and joy when we are able to preserve mutual love for each other, and we feel this comes from the presence of Jesus in our midst.

But sometimes we found it hard to have mutual love in the morning. Some of us, for example, would wake up on the wrong side of the bed and begin the day in a kind of grouchy mood. When this happened it took us a while before we would all start to love in concrete ways and have the unity that we all wanted. It was at this time that we decided to pray all together in the morning. Even though it would be a sacrifice for those who didn't have to get up so early—with twelve of us, we had several different schedules—we decided that we should come together at 6:30 A.M., shortly before the first child had to leave for school.

Almost immediately we noticed the difference: those who were rather sluggish seemed to have more life and those who were a bit grumpy became more cheerful. As soon as we finished praying, we all greeted each other with a kiss and a smile. In this way we found that we were able to begin to love right at the start of the day, and to strive together to have Jesus in our midst, as he promised. And his presence among us is the greatest fruit of praying together.

M. and L. D.

Family Security

Sam: I was approaching twenty-one years of employment with the same company, making a good salary, and receiving good benefits. I felt very secure in spite of rumors that our department was going to close, but last summer that was exactly what happened.

All the staff of our department was assigned to a placement center for sixty days. During the first few days, I had an interview within the company. The interview went well, but as I walked out the door, a little voice from inside kept saying, "What that department is involved in is unacceptable to your beliefs." This reaction caught me completely by surprise, for I had worked in the very same division twenty-one years before and thought nothing of it. But I had since made the choice to put God in the first place in my life, and I couldn't turn my back on him now.

I talked it over with my wife, Rita, and we agreed that it was not God's will for me to take this particular job. The next day I turned down the offer that would have given me the same pay, benefits and security to which we had become accustomed. As we watched twenty years of hard work and dreams—all our security—vanish before our eyes, the whole family turned to God.

Rita: When Sam and I sat down to discuss the job offer, the idea of holding on to the security was tempting, but we really had the feeling that God was asking us to say yes to him by turning our backs on material worries and really placing ourselves in his hands, trusting in his providence.

Before Sam's job situation changed, we had made the decision to move to another house that had been vacant about ten years. These plans had progressed to the point that we could no longer change them; furthermore, we would have to start renovations to get the house ready to move into before school started—at least that was my idea. Sam and I really plunged into the work—putting it as our number one priority.

Soon, however, the whole family was feeling the pressure: both job and housing situations were disturbing the children. Sam and I realized that we had to put aside our idea and timetable in order to maintain a loving atmosphere at home. This meant living each present moment and trying to keep the girls' activities as normal as possible under the circumstances. When people asked when we were going to move we truthfully answered: "Only God knows."

These circumstances have certainly given us a lot of things to pray about within the family. Being that the children have gotten older and that we have different schedules, it is a challenge to find the time to pray together. Usually in the car on the way to school, we take a moment to turn over our concerns to God, praying specifically for the things we need as well as for other people. In contrast to the bustle of getting ready to leave, the atmosphere in the car during those moments when we pray together is peaceful and serene. It helps us to focus our day in trying to do God's will.

On one occasion we met a mother and her child from the same school that our youngest daughter attends. During our conversation, we learned that she had just moved into the area and was struggling to work, go to school, and raise two children as a single parent. We listened to her with love and offered her our help. Moments like these have really been a blessing for us because they help us come out of ourselves.

Sam: Even though I continue to juggle job hunting and house restoration, I try always to remember that the most important thing is to love in every present moment.

One morning recently, I was preparing to work on the

house when the phone rang. At the other end was our youngest child, frantic, half crying, half trying to talk. After she calmed down, she explained that all her homework had been left at the other house. Without hesitation, I dropped everything and made the one-hour round trip to the house and then to her school. I then waited in the parking lot as the children marched from the church back into school. The look on her face was enough to make the rest of my day one of the most productive yet.

S. and R. H.

The Move

Maryann: When Herb and I met, we were both already involved with the Focolare movement. We felt that its spirituality of unity which we had tried to live as individuals, would be our source of strength as a couple, even though we came from different churches. After four and a half years of marriage and three children, we are even more certain that this spirituality is the key to solving many difficulties that arise in our married life.

Recently we purchased a new home. I knew that with three babies, it would be difficult to accomplish many of the jobs that needed to be done before we moved, and after only one month, I was getting anxious and starting to nag Herb. I kept questioning him about why it was taking him so long to do certain jobs. After I did this a number of times, Herb became upset with me and told me quite emphatically to stop it. Although I knew that I was wrong, my ego is strong and I became angry. My natural inclination when feeling hurt is to shut myself off for days, but I reminded myself that to love one another so as to have Christ among us is more important than anything else. We apologized to each other and decided that it was time to start over again.

Starting again implies forgiving the other and forgiving oneself, and it has always given me freedom to go beyond myself. It is in that moment that I make a conscious decision to put everything—the hurt, the anger, and the anxiety—behind me and to begin again to love. Peace returns and I feel happy again.

An experience that reminded me of the importance of starting again involved putting plastic insulation on the bedroom windows for the winter. Herb is usually very precise and measures things very carefully, but this time he just took the scissors and started cutting. It seemed to me to be very careless and wasteful. Being somewhat shocked at his approach, I let him know how I felt. I, of course, assumed that he would change his ways right away. But when I saw that he didn't, I became furious and stormed out of the bedroom, refusing to help. As I sat in the other room fuming, I felt as if Jesus within me was asking, "Do you love me more than this?" I answered, "Yes, Lord." I soon felt the freedom to let go of my ideas and had the courage to get up and go apologize. At the same moment, Herb came out of the bedroom to apologize as well. We both felt the joy of starting again to live united.

Herb: I belong to the Episcopal Church. I was first attracted to the spirituality of unity because I saw Christians trying to live out their faith in daily life. The fact that many of these people were Roman Catholics did not create problems for me. Together with them, I was able to deepen my own faith despite the differences in our background. The reason for this is that unity calls us to look for what binds us together rather than what divides us.

When I met Maryann, I was at a stage in my life where I felt that God was calling me to be married—that this was his way for me to go toward him. Thus it was more important to find someone who was also seeking to go to God together than to choose someone from my own Church. I entrusted my search to God because I felt it to be his will. His answer was Maryann.

Our vision of ourselves as a couple has been based upon a belief that it is his will for us to progress in unity. Being united in Christ is the foundation, the bedrock, of our relationship and our love for each other.

Maintaining unity is not easy, and the experiences that I

recall most vividly are those in which there is a division and things have to be rebuilt. Sometimes it is something simple, like quarreling over what each of us should be doing when the kids won't take the nap that they need because we have guests coming later. At these times it is enough to acknowledge that our disagreement was ridiculous and start again. At other times, however, it is necessary to examine and unmask the real motives behind our actions first, but to start again just the same.

For example, with regard to our new home, we only had about three weeks to actually prepare it before the move. During that time, we managed to paint, to have the floors varnished, and to bring over a number of boxes. Maryann was planning to unload little by little the contents of the cupboards and closets and to set them up in the new home, so that when moving day came all would be in order and very little unpacking would need to be done. However, through various circumstances we had not achieved everything which we had set out to do. The evening before moving we were taking some things over to the new house. Maryann was intent on getting some cleaning done there, but I was more concerned that we should be ready for the movers who would be arriving between eight and nine the following morning. My perception was that we still had plenty more to pack and that what Maryann wanted to do was not the right thing at that moment.

As we talked, I tried to persuade her that we had to stop thinking about being ready to move in and instead concentrate on being ready to move out. But my tone and attitude were not charitable at all: it seemed to me that Maryann had no understanding of the situation and was not even listening to me. By the time we arrived at the new house, Maryann had decided not to move from the car. I was left to unload the car myself. I was hurt because Maryann had accused me of being the reason for her not having the time to do what she felt was necessary.

As I unloaded, my first inclination was to just dump things and go. However, some things, like the freezer which had to be reconnected, needed to be put away and I realized it would not be loving to ignore doing it. Then I realized that the most important part of being ready to move was to be united and that I had to do my part to mend the pieces. First, I acknowledged within myself that there certainly must have been failings on my part for Maryann to accuse me the way she did. Even though I saw the circumstances in a different way, I felt ready to ask for forgiveness. So, when I got back in the car, I shared these feelings with Maryann with all the love that I could. Things began to change and by the end of the evening we had restored our unity and we worked together preparing for the following day.

I remember the moving day going very well, even though there were additional problems such as clearing the snow that had fallen overnight. I felt that because we had taken the steps to go beyond our own worries and preoccupations, we were able to do things out of love for one another and the movers. As a result, everything seemed to fall into place. At the end of the day we felt the peace and joy that comes from being united.

M. and H. P.

My Daughter's Friend

I am the father of seven daughters, and together with my wife, we have always tried to maintain a spirit of mutual love in our family. And when we have failed to do this, we have tried as soon as possible to begin again, seeing each other as if for the first time, trying not to remember whatever fault caused the break between us.

This effort over many years has contributed toward the formation of our children. It's true that they are often attracted to all the same things of others their age, but they seem to have learned to be sensitive to the divine; such that when something goes against that, they avoid it to a great degree.

I really think they are beautiful girls with very transparent souls that have been nourished with the presence of God in the family. So when something threatens them, I sometimes react very strongly. Some would call this being over protective, and I have been excessive in this regard. But there is a lot to protect, and much to protect them from.

My overreaction was illustrated in an experience I had over a period of time with one of my high school daughters. From the time she was in eighth grade, she seemed to be drifting into things that I found potentially offensive to her goodness. The music she preferred, the films and TV shows she would have watched if I had allowed her, were indicative of this.

She had a few friends that I thought had the same

inclinations, and I began to unconsciously assign the cause to them—especially one of them. In fact, she began talking and associating with this girl almost exclusively.

They ended up both going to the same high school, so things intensified. Little by little, I got more and more intolerant. I would scream at her when she talked on the phone too much. I would accuse her of becoming boy crazy. I knew I was wrong, but my feelings would get the best of me momentarily and I would say these things before I could control them.

At a certain point, I knew I had to change. This was not love. As much as I didn't want my daughter to slide away from the love of God, I myself was sliding away from it. It was like a landslide, in fact.

The love that Jesus taught made no exclusions. I was excluding my daughter's friend. I knew inside that I should love my "neighbor's" daughter as I would love my own. It wasn't a matter of feelings. It was a matter of love. Real, tough love.

I took the step. I began to ask my daughter to have her friend over, even to stay overnight. I would ask her friend about her family and school. She started feeling a little more comfortable and willing to come over. She still liked the kind of music that I found non-constructive to say the least, but I set that aside in order to maintain openness and communication.

I still was not happy that my daughter spent so much time with this one friend. I tried to encourage her to spend time with others too. So when it was time for the annual father/daughters' dance at her school, I happily agreed to go in order to get her a little more into the setting of other friends.

My older daughter was going too, so we had it all planned and were ready. My daughter's friend wasn't going, because her father was out of town.

The day of the dance, however, my daughter asked if she could skip it. It seemed that her friend wanted company, and my daughter wanted to accommodate her. I felt

38

frustrated. But I tightened up, and just thought for a while, trying to figure out what to do.

Finally, I realized that the best thing to do in order to love my daughter's friend as I would my own daughter, was to invite her too to the dance. After all, her father was away and couldn't bring her, so I could fill in as her father.

That's what I did, and she came.

The dance was another exercise in loving as Jesus would. I'm not the dancing type, but I became one. You would have thought I did this every week. At times I was dancing with all three of them at once. At a certain point, I danced with my daughter's friend. I told her, "for tonight you're my daughter."

The moment came for pictures to be taken. The emotional side of me made me project into the future, imagining that in my ancient years, I could look at this picture of my two daughters with me and remember a beautiful experience, doing something that made them happy. But when our turn came to pose, I immediately insisted that the friend be part of the picture. She loved it, and I was even happier—emotionally, too.

Since then, things have been going well. I've gotten to know the friend well, and I found that in some cases, I had really exaggerated in my mind about her inclinations. And allowing a freedom of movement for her and my daughter, I've helped to create an atmosphere that allows my daughter to be a good influence on her friend.

F. E.

Nothing is Impossible For God

When I married Nick four years ago I acquired four grown step children and since then six grandchildren. It was not a close family and the relationships with each of them has presented unique challenges. Some of the things that Chiara Lubich has shared with us over the years about putting the gospel into practice have helped us greatly in knowing how to approach each of these relationships, and have also helped me support Nick in them, especially the ones that were somewhat divided. So, how does someone re-enter a relationship which is divided, overcome hurt feelings and have the courage to start loving again? At one instance Chiara says, "Where there is no love put love, always be the first to love, love always." This idea motivated me to put aside my own ideas, thoughts and feelings and helped me find the courage to start loving again.

Last November a significant incident happened with our son Ralph with whom, as of then, we had spoken perhaps once or twice the whole year. A year earlier he had married and now his anniversary as well as his birthday and Christmas were approaching. Nick and I sat down to see what possible options there were to do something for Ralph. How would Jesus love if he were in our place? The first thing we thought was that we could send an anniversary card. We didn't want to impose on him; we wanted to respect the distance that he had placed between us. We sent Ralph a card and Nick wrote a note in it. For his birthday Nick asked me about getting him a couple of shirts as a gift. This meant adding another item to our really crowded agenda, to take my previously made plans and give them up in order to pursue this new one.

That first Saturday in December at the mall was wall to wall shoppers. But, the first store we entered was filled with a great selection of shirts in exactly the right size. We felt the closeness of God. Somehow we had the certainty of being in his will. That evening we dropped off the presents on the way to a company Christmas party. The initial reception was kind of awkward but as we visited with them our relationship grew more relaxed and just as we were leaving Nick spontaneously asked if they would like to have dinner with us sometime. There was an uneasy silence which seemed to last a long time, then Ralph accepted our invitation and chose a date two weeks later.

In two weeks we all met kind of nervously at the local

pizza place and again it started kind of awkwardly. After a short time though, we were talking and laughing. When we left the restaurant afterward to walk to our car it seemed as if it had been the most beautiful evening we had ever experienced. Again we felt the closeness of God and I said to Nick, "That was not just great, it was fun." Nick then looked at me and said, "You know that's the most I've talked to my son in five years." We felt that if we just try to love a little bit, God can do great things.

Recently, we spent four hours with another one of our children who had called us. She was very upset with her marriage. We went over to see her immediately, hoping to put love where things were very difficult. While we were there her husband arrived and we found ourselves in the middle of a division. We knew it would be easier to leave, but at that moment we decided to stay, desiring to at least be instruments of love. We tried to listen and to say something only when it would be in some way love for them. There were moments where Nick was able to offer some of the ideas of trying to put charity into practice, some of the ideas that have made our marriage much more peaceful. Their situation is not yet resolved but as Nick and I drove home we spontaneously said to each other that we needed to pray more.

Humanly speaking we could easily be discouraged and we could decide not to put forth the effort in going and visiting and spending time with our children anymore. We could say that we're too busy or that the relationships are too difficult, reasoning that it's impossible anyway, or that it will never work. It's always tempting to think this way but we've already experienced the fruits when we've tried to love even just a little bit. God seems to give such reward. We believe that if we are able to put love in these situations then God will suggest a solution and will bring it to a completion that's according to his will. We know that nothing is impossible for God.

L. N.

"The family is . . . a repository, a jewel, a mystery of love"
(14)
In her talk, Chiara Lubich explains how God thinks of the
family as an "intertwining of relationships of love." In the
next five experiences, we see how the "mystery of love"
takes in parents, children, and grandparents.

Our Extended Family

My husband and I realized some years ago that we are part of a larger spiritual family. We have tried to put the gospel into practice by becoming more aware of who our neighbor is and to see Jesus in each person. Jesus was asked, "But when did we see you, Lord?" And he replied, "When I was hungry, you gave me food; naked and you clothed me; homeless and you took me in. . . . "

So during the past five years we have opened our home to our new found sisters and brothers who need a place to stay. Sometimes they stay for a short time; other times it is longer.

When we were first presented with someone who needed a place to stay, we still had two children at home. If we, as a family, decided to take this person in, where would we put her? What would our children say? But before we could even begin discussing such details, our two children told us that they would not mind sharing a room so that our friend could have her own room. Their offer surprised us since only recently they had received their own rooms. This seemed to be a sign that the way we were trying to live was having a positive effect on our family.

Some of our other children who are married have since started to open their homes when there is an expressed need as well. We can see during holidays a desire by our family to share what we have with others who may not have a family close by or who cannot afford all the fixings that go into a holiday meal.

By now our children have become self-sufficient and moved away. Their moving left us with a lot of spare room in our home, so we considered selling the house and moving into something smaller. But God had other plans for us.

Recently, my ninety-two-year-old mother-in-law moved in with us. She and I never had a close relationship. Her moving in has been a difficult adjustment for all of us, but especially for her with her medical problems and new surroundings. At first I was all for her coming to live with us, but later on the reality of it all hit me.

Shortly after she arrived, my husband had to travel out of state, so I needed to take some time off from work to care for her. That meant bathing and dressing her and helping her with meals. The first morning I was very nervous, but I told myself that this was Jesus and that I was helping him. I could see that trying to put the gospel into practice was having an effect on her too. When I put her to bed that night, she embraced me and told me that she loved me.

Our whole family takes turns "grandmother-sitting" when we need to go out now. Again it is a confirmation that Christian love has become a true way of life for our entire family.

M. R.

Nothing Matters But to Love

One Sunday my brother, his wife and I decided to pay an unexpected visit to my mother. When we arrived at the apartment, my mom came to the door in a wobbling manner. She let us in and rushed back to sit down. We followed quite concerned and began frantically asking her what was wrong. I could see that this was confusing her so I waited a few moments and asked her again, in a calm tone. I realized how frightening all this was for her; however, she was in poor condition and it was clear that we had to move her out that very day.

I confronted her with our decision carefully and delicately, wanting to allow her to maintain her dignity. At first she resisted and I was tempted to say, "It doesn't matter how you feel, we have to take you with us." But, instead of reacting that way, I took her hand and proceeded to describe the room she would be occupying in our home and I told her how we were all waiting for Grandma's cooking. She smiled, nodded, and said, "Do you really want me to cook for your family?" This cost me. I thought, "I can't give up my kitchen!" In a flash I remembered, "Whatsoever you do to the least, you do to me." I answered sincerely, "Yes, we are waiting." Then, realizing that I had no time to prepare the room in advance, I began to feel overwhelmed. What could I do? I found a moment alone, called home and explained the situation to my son. Before I could even finish he calmly said, "Don't worry, we'll take care of it." In that moment I sensed God's personal love.

My mother had accumulated many articles over the years and I would have liked to just discard everything and take her home. But, remembering that I had to love Jesus in her, I patiently went through what we could consulting her about everything. I also explained that whatever we couldn't take that day, the boys would come back for with their van. She left very peacefully and when we arrived at home she was welcomed with a party from the children. They even put up a welcome sign with balloons. It was a joyful moment and an experience of the hundredfold promised in the gospel for those who do things for Jesus.

As time passed by I realized more and more the depth of this new responsibility. My home suddenly was no longer mine; now I had company that I didn't invite, meals I didn't plan. I felt invaded, and I felt resentful towards my sisters and brother. After all, they were all older than I, why me? Each time I realized these judgments were wrong and corrected my attitude. Doing so I understood better that this was God's will for me.

My mom lived with us for two years, until the morning she had a stroke. I remember that day in one breath saying,

"God can't you even spare me this?" and in the next breath I was saying, "I know and believe that this too is your personal love for my mother and me." She was left paralyzed on the entire left side of her body. After a while the hospital informed me that my mother had to go to a nursing home. I was now by default her surrogate, the member of the family who makes all the decisions since the patient is not capable. I felt cornered and incapable. They told me that I had to find a nursing home and I had to apply for Medicaid. Once again I angrily questioned my position, "Why do I have to do all the work?" I remember saying to my husband, "Doesn't mother have any other children? I feel like I'm the only child." And he said, "In a sense you are, you're the child chosen by God." My husband's words gave me courage to continue. He was very supportive. And so, I turned all this over to God and out of love for him I was able to take each step as it came.

I began filling out the applications for nursing homes and began visiting all the facilities on my list. When I went to the Medicaid office, I put aside my anxieties and went to the caseworker trying just to love. Aware that it could take months to obtain a medicaid number, I had to keep reminding myself to do nothing but love moment after moment. The caseworker reviewed everything and looked up at me saying, "you have done my job, this is complete." I left convinced that if I do all my part, God is never outdone in generosity.

As I visited the different facilities I had to continuously overcome my grief and guilt about leaving my mom there. I found one near my home and thought this would be ideal. I said a little prayer believing all things are possible with God. The following week I received a phone call from that facility saying there was a bed. It also seemed that since my file was complete and there was a bed available, the supervisor would be able to issue the medicaid number. When I hung up the phone I began to cry. I was so struck again by God's personal love.

My mother was moved to her new home and when it

came time to leave her there alone for the first time, I felt as if I was abandoning her. And even after many months had gone by, each time I had to leave her it was a suffering.

On the first day of her arrival at the nursing home, I had to see the social director for instructions about proper clothing. Her garments had to open in the back but it was Friday, and the outlet where the clothing was sold was closed for the weekend. So I went home and took her petticoats and dresses and began to alter them. I was sewing all weekend. One of my sisters came to visit and I asked for her help. I was stunned when she refused. My first impulse was to scream at her and remind her of all that I had endured for months. I felt justified for a moment, but then realized that I shouldn't judge her and I renewed my determination to love to the end. I made it to entertain my sister all the while repeating: "for you Jesus, for you."

During the months that followed I had a conflict with one of the aides at the home. The tension between us was mounting. One day she told me to buy crocheted slippers for my mother. All the rules and regulations were beginning to get to me and her attitude really annoyed me. I wanted to tell her to leave me alone, but a voice inside kept telling me to love and understand how she was feeling. So I put my anger aside and went shopping that very day to five different department stores. I was unable to find any and I was reluctant to go back and face her with this news.

I arrived at the nursing home the next day hoping I wouldn't see her. However, she found me. I told her I didn't have the slippers and she replied, "Can you make them?" "No way." She persisted and said, "Then find someone who can." I was about to explode, but again I thought: "put yourself in her shoes, try to understand her." I made a pact with God at this point to do everything possible out of love for this woman. I left and found someone to crochet the slippers and then I brought them back to the aide. From then on instead of avoiding her I went out of my way to find ways to serve and understand her.

I began to look forward to every encounter with her.

Sometimes I just listened to her complaints, sometimes I tried to console her and I always had to be patient with her. As a result a relationship began. She let down her defenses and began to share her life with me. We became very close. Ironically she never used the slippers but every time I see them in the drawer they're a reflection to me of the love that has remained.

One day while trying to cut my mother's hair and hold her up at the same time, I became very frustrated because she wasn't cooperating. Suddenly she looked into my eyes and all I could see was Jesus. From that moment, my suffering was turned into joy.

It has been over a year since my mother was admitted into the nursing home. These experiences continue as the days go by. Others who don't understand my reasoning suggest quite often to me to pray for God to take her. But I am no longer fearful of the future or worried about how long this might go on. In fact, the experience of visiting and leaving the nursing home seems no longer draining. I am not distracted by external things anymore. Nothing matters but to love.

J. D.

A Tense Situation

Patty: When Steve and I got married twenty years ago, I had little idea of what life was going to be like. I thought our faith was strong faith, yet we were basically Sunday Catholics. Having been a student most of my life, I was convinced that hard work and study were going to be the foundation of success. So I did well in school and managed to finish graduate school two years after we got married. However, I was not happy with myself and with the world around me.

Then some years ago my mother passed away. It was a tremendous suffering. I spent a lot of time in church meditating on why God had taken her away so soon. According to my plans, my parents were to come to live with us, being that I was away from my homeland for over twelve years and never had the time, the money or a visa to go back to visit them. My mother's death made me quite depressed.

Steve was very supportive, but we were pretty much alone since our families were far away overseas. Two years later, before Christmas, we decided to join a Bible study group in our parish. We were immediately welcomed by the group. That was the first time I experienced the warmth of a God-centered support group. My journey of faith really began at that time.

With our first child, God's mercy became very tangible, and our second followed soon after, about the time that we moved to Maryland. Being in a new town and having lost the close ties with our previous parish, I once again became lonely. Through a friend we got to know the Focolare movement and its spirituality based on Jesus' prayer for unity.

Steve and I were both so affected by it that we began to live the spirituality of unity at home and in our work places. It helped us to slowly clarify our priorities and values. Going to church was no longer something we did just to fulfill our obligation; it was a visit to Jesus.

Around this time my father came to live with us. I had already started to try to have a loving attitude for every person who came my way. But the most challenging one turned out to be my father. We have big differences in our perceptions and we both feel we are right. Our relationship began deteriorating day by day. Helped by Steve and our Christian lifestyle, bit by bit I tried to re-establish peace with him. Today, we get along much better. In building unity, I see I have to die to myself a little, but instead of having the "poor me" feeling, I experience a hundredfold of joy.

Steve: Ever since my father-in-law moved in with us there has been a lot of tension between the two of us. He considers me to be too "Americanized" and he does not view the world the same way as I do. I have often felt that he was at times too eager to try to influence me to do things his way, including the way to take care of my two-year-old son.

One day at the dinner table my son was alone in his high chair for a moment and started leaning forward in an attempt to grasp something on the table. My father-in-law jumped up from his chair, ran toward my son and dramatically restrained him. Feelings of resentment rose up inside me; it seemed to be another example of him wanting to do things his way. I rose from my chair, raised my voice in a very irritable way, and forcibly took my son away from him.

My resentments prevented me from seeing his act of love towards my son. Not until my wife talked to me later did I realize how much my father-in-law was hurt by my insensitivity. My wife's support allowed me to admit in my heart that it was my fault and I took the first step to make things up between us by talking to him about his favorite subject—my son.

The whole family became united again because of my wife's support, which helped me to take the first step. In family situations I sometimes fail to see Jesus in the others, but even when I fail I know that I can always start again.

Another day my wife and her father had some serious disagreements, and it appeared that they had stopped speaking to each other. It so happened that I was myself under quite a bit of stress at work due to a number of pressing problems. Since my wife and her father's differences appeared to be between *them*, I wasn't about to interfere. But, in reality, due to my preoccupation with work, I was reluctant to do what love demanded for either my wife or my father-in-law at that moment.

I prayed about it, however, and decided to take the initiative to go to his room and make an effort to listen to him without taking sides. He started talking and said how unhappy he was because we didn't care for him, and that he may want to leave us and return to his home. I kept listening, trying to make him feel accepted and understood.

When I left his room that morning, I could see that he was much happier because he felt that I was trying to share his burden. The most surprising thing was that I felt much better myself; I almost forgot my own anxieties and problems at work.

I experienced that peace comes to us when we become peacemakers in our own way. We must try to be united as a family and have Christ in our midst by being available and bringing peace to each other.

Patty: Three years ago, I became pregnant with our third child. Our original plan for a third child was to adopt a two-year-old from overseas; perhaps a child who would be toilet trained and would be closer in age to our two daughters. But God wanted to give us a child in his way. We accepted the pregnancy with great joy. The first few visits to the doctor were a suffering because they strongly recommended me to undergo a test to see if the baby was retarded. I repeatedly refused their suggestions. However, I started to build up a lot of fear that the baby might really be abnormal. It was another opportunity for me to struggle through the acceptance of God's will. If the baby would be retarded, I trusted that God would give us the grace to handle it. When the baby arrived quite normal, we were all overjoyed.

In trying to put this spirituality of unity into practice in our family, I've discovered that this life overflows in various ways to other families we're in contact with. For example, last December our children's music teacher organized a chorus to perform at the mall. One of the songs was rather inappropriate. The verses seemed to ridicule certain types of persons. I thought this indirectly teaches the children that it's all right to mock people. As I was thinking about the best way to approach the school about this, I found out the children already started using these verses among themselves. So I called the principal and discussed the matter with him. Then I talked to a few other parents about my concern. They all agreed with me, but didn't think they could do anything about it. They too then decided to speak with the principal. Two days later, the principal and the music teacher decided to eliminate the song. I was happy to see this action taken but deep in my heart I knew that it was God who gave me the courage to speak up.

P. and S. K.

Caring For Our Mother-in-Law

Filial love towards parents I think can be extended also to parents-in-law. This, at least, has been my experience with my mother-in-law.

My mother-in-law is ninety-four years of age, a widow, half-blind, has undergone surgery on the spinal column, and is confined to a wheel chair. Until recently she lived with my family in our home.

She would normally find herself alone at home during the weekdays for the whole day or part of it because everyone in the family either goes to school or works. When we would come home in the evening it was always a happy occasion for her. We would all make an effort to show our love in small things. One of our girls, for example, would play and joke with her and at times even sleep close to her in the same bed.

During the night when she would have her usual asthma attacks and experience difficulty breathing, my wife and I would get up and stay close to her just to make her feel that she was not alone in her suffering. In some moments, we would pray together to take her mind a bit away from her passing difficulty.

Early this year my mother-in-law entered the hospital, and her condition was very serious. She was having difficulty breathing, again caused by asthma. Her heart and lungs were weak and she could hardly eat at all. In the hospital the doctor asked my wife whether or not she wanted her mother to continue with the life support system to prolong her life. We decided that there was no further need for the application of this measure because we were ready to go along with God's will, and besides we did not want to see her suffer even more.

At that time other members of my wife's family, including her only living brother and his wife, both of whom had not been seen for years, as well as some of my own relatives, came to give some moral support. The doctor gave my mother-in-law a fifty percent chance of surviving. Our uncle was impressed with the way our children were looking after his sister, each one taking turns on a rotation basis to watch over her. He considered it quite unnatural for a twenty-four-year-old boy, for example, to stay with his grandmother the whole night in the hospital.

Even though she was given a very slim chance of survival, my mother-in-law overcame the crisis surprisingly. But after a week, she had a heart attack, and this time the doctor said that nothing could be done to alleviate her condition and we would just have to wait for the inevitable. Again, miraculously she overcame it. After a few more days, gangrene started to develop in her right leg and our family was placed in a dilemma: amputate or let her pass away in a very painful way. Finally, we made the decision to go ahead with the operation, again putting our trust and confidence in God, believing that it was his will to do so. I remember I was with my wife in the hospital, and we were praying. The doctor had told us to wait for the results for at least an hour, so we were all surprised to see her after less than an hour, coming from the operating room half awake and seeming to have overcome all dangers.

She has been placed in a convalescent hospital now and my wife, who has since quit her job, has been taking constant care of her. Our children take turns to see her.

There have been times when I would ask her how she feels; she answers that she would prefer to die rather than to suffer continuously in such a situation. I would like to help her to fully accept her condition, and I often feel a God-given strength to tell her that we must continue to accept it and profit from these sufferings as a way to prepare for something beautiful, possibly for her entrance into heaven. She responds quite favorably and agrees to do just that. Recently she asked me to call our priest friend so that she could make another confession, perhaps the last that she would ever make, and receive communion.

She added finally, to console me, that she has seen the beauty of our family and she is ready to die in peace knowing that God has taken good care of each one of us during her lifetime. To me, it was a confirmation of the love that she must have felt from the members of our family.

We do not know how long she will still remain here on earth, or how much suffering everyone in our family will have to bear watching her go through this experience. But that is secondary now because I am certain that, with all our prayers and those of our friends, her suffering here on earth and that of the family will not go without its merit or reward from God.

T. W.

Beyond Words

My father was a quiet individual who spent most of his life working as a businessman. As was more typical in days past my mom was responsible for the house and for the children and my father was responsible for financially supporting us. He was never an active part of my life when I was growing up and there was little communication between us. This pattern continued into my adult life because I have always lived very far away from him. There was never animosity or anger between us, but I felt an emotional void in our relationship and I never knew how to fill this void with something meaningful and lasting.

When I would go for visits over the years, because we lived so far away, it was always an occasion of huge family gatherings and there never seemed to be time to share with him the things that were important in my life. When there was time, I never could find a way to begin because my Dad did not like to talk much about feelings. As his health began to fail a few years ago I became more distressed about our relationship, and I wanted very much to fill this void between us before he died.

Last December it seemed clear that he did not have many more weeks, or even possibly days to live. I left immediately for California in a state of nervousness and fatigue. This was my last chance to have a meaningful conversation with my Dad, to tell him things that I felt he should know about my life. But how would I find a way this time? I found the answer in the gospel and in the spirituality of unity that I had started to live in contact with the Focolare movement. What I had to do were just concrete acts of love for my father whenever I could. I had to put myself in his shoes in every moment: if my father wanted to talk, I would talk. But if he did not want to talk then my love had to be words enough.

My father was in a hospital bed at home and he was too weak to do anything for himself. Often he was confused and was in and out of reality. I fed him, washed him, reassured him and sat on the edge of his bed so that I would be available to him if he wanted to say anything. I tried to do everything in a way that my Dad would not feel a burden, and would maintain his dignity, because I knew that it must have been difficult for him to have his daughter take care of all his personal needs. One night when he couldn't sleep because of his constant coughing and hallucinating, I asked him if I could pray out loud. He did not answer, but as I prayed he slowly became less agitated and fell asleep for a short time.

One day we had him transported to the hospital for a blood transfusion. As I sat with him he was very coherent and shared with me that he was ready to die. He felt he had lived a good life but that now he was a burden and that therefore he was ready to leave. I told him that I was very happy to hear that he was prepared, and that it made it easier for all of us to let him go. I spoke to him a little about paradise and he seemed very at peace. It was a real moment of grace between us.

That night it was my turn again to stay with him through the night. I was extremely tired and my Dad called out for me to do something for him every ten minutes. I started to feel dizzy every time I got up from the chair and I felt that I couldn't really continue. At a critical moment I prayed that God would give me the physical and emotional strength to see this to the end. The next time he needed my help I smiled, cared for him with more patience in my movements, and felt at peace.

The following morning I had to return to my home and family. Knowing I would not see him again alive, I wanted to find a few moments alone with him to say goodbye. Right before I was to leave I went to his bed; he was awake, but his mind was not clear. As I started speaking to him he looked at me and I could see the understanding come back into his eyes. I told him that I was leaving and would not see him again in this life, but that I knew we would be together in a more beautiful life someday. He smiled. Then I told him that I was very happy that we had been able to have these days together, and that I was sorry that I couldn't have done more for him. He thanked me and said, "You did a lot for me, but most important, you made me feel loved."

On the plane home, I realized that the void between my father and me had been filled, unity now took its place. I had not spoken with him about my life, but I had tried to show him what I was trying to do each day of my life with my actions. He understood and shared that understanding with me, which meant more to me than all the conversations in the world.

R. W.

Part III

COMMITMENT, LIGHT AND JOY

What is the relationship between the family and prayer? In Part I we learned that prayer originates from the family, families are the first "school of prayer," as the U.S. Bishops affirm in their document "Sharing the Light of Faith: National Catechetical Directory for Catholics of the United States." In Part II, we have seen that it is through their relationship with God that family members find the strength to serve one another.

In this section, prayer, meditation, reflection on experience, and the Mass, the great action of the Church in unity, emerge as central and nurturing components of family life. The life of a family so nurtured, however, naturally extends to others. As Chiara Lubich points out with her example of interconnected containers of water, "Prayer is basically a personal concern, but . . . when we are elevated to [God], also the others are elevated." The social impact of families whose lives are rooted in prayer will be described and witnessed in the shared, living experiences.

We will start this section with one family's experience as the recipient and as the agent of divine providence. From there, we will enter into the impact of families, recollected in prayer, on their neighbors who face some of the most serious social issues of our day.

The holy journey which these families have chosen to follow radiates commitment, light, and joy, fruits of living in unity.

"Prayer in the family . . . is exceptionally effective" (18).
The following experience shows in capsule form how a
family centered on its relationship to God turns naturally
to find God in its neighbors and shows how prayer is
reflected in daily actions becoming sacred actions.

Family Affairs

Last year's family vacation included a cross-country drive
to visit relatives in Los Angeles. One evening it was getting
very late and we decided to stop in Santa Rosa for the night.
Early the next morning, before continuing on we found a
local church and went to Mass together as we always do.
After Mass, as we were trying to figure out where to eat
breakfast, two women approached us and started to
compliment us on our nice family; they were touched to
see us all together there in church. One of them invited our
family of seven to her house for breakfast and although we
hesitated and tried to refuse politely we soon realized that
she was sincere and determined, so we accepted. While
eating together we spoke of our Filipino heritage. She
explained to us that her husband was stationed in the
Philippines and that they have many beautiful memories of
the Philippines and of the Filipino people.

When we got on the road again I realized that we had
saved at least thirty dollars by eating at this woman's house.
I was thinking about this when one of our children told us
that she needed to stop at one of the rest stations along the
highway. We exited at the next one. There we met a woman
who was stuck with no gas and no money. She was trying
to reach San Jose to start a new job the next day. We decided
together to help her. We gave her the money we had saved
so that she could reach her destination.

One strong experience we had was with another Filipino
family of eight children that we came to know through
friends of ours. When we met them Ann, the mother, had

just undergone very extensive cancer surgery and was bed-ridden. Bill, the father, worked nights and had to sleep during the day. Needless to say Ann was having a very difficult time and would entrust the various household chores like grocery shopping, cooking, housekeeping and laundry to one or another of the children, most of whom were very young.

We felt that we had met them at a very timely moment. We immediately developed a strong relationship with them. Since they had no immediate relatives in the area, my children and I would cook food for them, usually enough for several days. We would sing Ann some of her favorite songs, pray together with the whole family and once I even had the possibility of bringing a priest to visit Ann.

Often their children joined our family for a day of apple picking or a picnic in the park. The cancer eventually took Ann's life. We took it upon ourselves to make all the necessary arrangements as well as explaining everything to the children, who were in school when she died. They also received a lot of help from other families that we are in contact with throughout that period and afterwards. Although it has been several years since this experience, a very strong relationship has remained between our families, a bond of unity and the presence of Jesus.

T. and J. F.

"Prayer is the elevation of our souls to God, and when we are elevated to him, also the others are elevated" (15). Perhaps no one feels the need for "elevation" more than those who face such profound choices as adoption or abortion. The families who share the next two experiences found that their attempts to base their lives on the gospel led them to provide the material and spiritual lift for women in these difficult circumstances.

The Adoption

Betty: In the early years of our marriage when I first stopped working to stay home with our small children, I felt I had been cut off from the outside world. I looked very much forward to Frank coming home each day to tell me what had gone on at work. But I realized that he didn't enjoy telling me about his days as much as I enjoyed listening to him. He was tired when he got home and really wanted to leave his work behind when he walked in the door.

It was about this time that through friends I came to a deeper understanding of the gospel, especially its aspect of unity (cf. Jn 17). I realized that in order to build and maintain unity with Frank, I couldn't ask him to tell me all the details of his day. To love Jesus in him, I had to remain silent, expecting nothing. It was difficult at first and I felt even more cut off. But as time went on, I noticed that he started sharing the real essential things—relationships with his employees, his problems, and his successes. We had begun living out the gospel together at this point, trying to keep the presence of the risen Jesus in our midst as he promises in scripture (cf. Mt 18:20). We found ourselves calling each other several times a day, assuring the other of our commitment to putting the gospel into practice as we lived through our daily situations. Then, in the evenings, when we would share some of our difficulties, we would try to see how the presence of Jesus among us could help to transform them.

Frank: About a year ago, a situation came up where the unity between Betty and me became valuable in assisting another family.

I work with a woman I'll call Grace, whose two children are grown and soon to be moving out of the house. Being divorced, she realized that she would be lonely, and therefore she decided to adopt a baby.

One day I overheard her saying that she had found a baby girl. When I asked her about it, she said she had found the baby through a friend after she had "put out the word." I learned that the baby was living at a crack house, along with her mother and two brothers. When Grace went to get the baby, the mother agreed, but not without leaving her two boys with Grace as well.

I felt uncomfortable with what was going on, and I realized that this situation couldn't pass by without me trying to love everyone involved as Jesus had loved me.

Betty: Frank came home and explained what was happening. One of our major concerns was Grace's second thoughts about the boys. Because they were older and harder to handle, she wanted to return them to their mother. This would have put them right back into an atmosphere of drugs and neglect. The other main concern was that Grace was keeping this baby without a legal adoption.

Our first thought was to do something in which Grace would feel our concern and love. We knew that when she picked the children up, the baby was wearing only a diaper and the boys had only a pair of shorts each. So, together with our children, we went through their outgrown clothing, choosing the nicer things, folding them carefully, trying to keep in mind that we were doing this for Jesus in those children.

Frank: The next day I took the clothes to Grace. She was very happy and told me that they were exactly what she would have bought for the children if she only could have afforded it. We began to talk, and she was confused about what to do next. She knew it wasn't right to put the boys back in that house. When I suggested calling child welfare, she immediately refused because she knew that such an action would mean giving up the baby as well. She also feared that if the mother lost her government assistance she might retaliate against her in a violent way.

At the end of our conversation, which took place on a Friday, Grace had decided to keep the boys. She was still confused about how to handle the three kids, but knowing that I shared her concern she seemed more at peace. I suggested thinking about everything over the weekend, and then talking it over again on Monday. The thoughts and prayers of our whole family were with Grace and the children that weekend.

On Monday I wanted to look for Grace; instead she came to me smiling. Over the weekend, she had searched and found the grandmother of the children. The grandmother knew of her daughter's difficulty with drugs, but did not know where to find her. She had been worried about the children and was relieved to know that they were doing fine. She told Grace that she wanted to take the children but that Grace would be welcome to see them anytime.

Grace brings me news of the situation from time to time. The baby has medical problems and Grace helps the grandmother by taking her to the doctor and even assisting financially when she can. The mother of the children has also contacted Grace, thanking her for what she is doing. She told Grace that some day she would like to take the children back and care for them.

By living out the gospel that brings us into full union with God through mutual love, we have found a way to sanctity in the midst of the world, at home and at work. Our daily actions become sacred actions and we are able to be authentic Christians, living shoulder to shoulder with neighbors like Grace.

F. and B. K.

"The Best Gift You Could Get at Christmas!"

Frank: One night not long ago, the phone rang at our house. It was Michele, a seventeen-year-old student who was on my caseload. She was classified as a "juvenile delinquent" and had served a year's sentence with the rehabilitation agency where I work. A few months ago she moved into a foster home in the community.

"I'm pregnant," she said. "I need you to get money for an abortion." As her caseworker, I had only to request the funds and she could go ahead with the abortion. Not knowing what to say, I ignored her request, for I was sure there must be some other option. So, instead of answering her, I invited her to our home for dinner.

Emily: We remembered how the families in our area had assured us of their love from the moment they knew we were expecting our first child, and we wanted to show this same love to Michele. When she came to dinner, I asked how she had been feeling about all the symptoms of early pregnancy. We looked at pictures of fetal development, comparing her baby's development at five weeks to ours, since I was five months pregnant. We hardly mentioned abortion, and we treated her as we would any other young mother. A relationship began.

Later I asked my obstetrician if Michele could come to my next appointment and listen to her baby's heartbeat. He seemed to understand completely, but warned me that it might be difficult to find the heartbeat so early in the pregnancy. On the day of the visit, the nurse tried especially hard and after a long time we could hear a slow "pum-pum-pum-pum." Michele flushed, "That's not *my* heart, is it?" She was really excited and afterward kept talking about what she had heard. When we parted, she was very happy, smiling and waving as if we shared a great secret.

Frank: Soon after Michele asked me to help her get

money for the abortion I learned how many people were encouraging her to have it. My director called me to say that Michele shouldn't wait too long because soon it might be illegal for her to have an abortion in our state. A caseworker who worked with me was pregnant at the time and she told Michele that she was personally considering an abortion and that maybe they could go to the clinic together. Michele's foster mother told her that since Michele couldn't take care of herself, she could not possibly take care of a baby.

Dan, my immediate superior at the rehabilitation agency, and I were deeply concerned about Michele. We prayed that God would help us see what to do in this situation. Dan and I both felt that we had to share with Michele our views on abortion, and we did on separate occasions. I also took Michele to Birthright Counseling Services to discuss the options of keeping the baby or giving him or her up for adoption. These counselors also explained the different methods of abortion and the ramifications for her as well as her baby.

I knew that I could be putting my job on the line by helping Michele make the right decision about having her baby. The director wouldn't want our agency to become known by probation offices as an agency that discourages pregnant teenagers from having abortions since probation offices are the major funding sources of our agency. Also at one of our meetings at work, a colleague accused me of pressuring Michele. I told them that as a social worker, I was simply exposing Michele to all her options.

I made sure I was the one to take Michele to the clinic for her prenatal visits. When Michele came out one time, the clinic was beginning to show a video of an actual birth. Michele said she didn't want to see it, but I said I'd like to stay because I would be going through childbirth again soon with Emily and wanted to be prepared. Michele left the room for a minute or two and then came back and never took her eyes off the screen. On the way home she told me that she decided to keep the baby.

The next time I brought her to see her parole officer, he asked to see her alone. When I came back into the room, the parole officer said, "I was afraid Michele was feeling pressured into making this decision. But now I see that she's so genuinely happy that this must be what she really wants to do."

Emily: What a joy Michele's decision was for Frank and me! But soon we saw that we needed to love with deeds and not just talk about it. I understood that this was not just a concern for Frank at his job but one for our whole family. First, Michele needed maternity clothes, so as I grew out of mine, I gave them to her. Then I was sure someone from Birthright or her foster mother or a female caseworker, or even her own mother would offer to be her labor partner and go with her to childbirth classes, but no one came forward. As time went on, it became obvious that I should be the one. Another problem was that Michele was not treated well at her foster home and often missed meals. On class nights, she sometimes came back to our home for dinner. Finally Michele decided not to give the baby up for adoption; she wanted to keep the baby with her.

When we invited friends to a Christmas party in our house, we told them about Michele who was expecting and asked if they might want to bring a gift for the new baby. The response was more than we ever expected. People brought new clothing and toys, as well as whole wardrobes of baby clothes, a changing table, playpen, blankets, and similar things. Michele couldn't come to the party, but it was beautiful to see the joy it brought people to give just a pure gift, without ever seeing for whom it was. Michele came over later in the evening; I had never seen her so happy as when we looked at everything together. She couldn't understand how all these people who didn't even know her could be so generous.

A week before Christmas Michele gave birth to a baby boy, and the look on her face told me he would always be loved. The night they came home from the hospital, they stayed at our house. She was tired, but full of wonder,

66

concern, and gentleness for her son. When I got up in the morning I saw the two of them fast asleep together, Michele's arm protecting her new baby. Then she told me how she cried in the hospital, thinking, "He's so beautiful, he doesn't deserve a mother like me." Over and over she told us what a gift he was: "Like the best gift you could get at Christmas, but one you never get tired of."

Since that time Michele has changed. She wanted to cooperate with Frank's agency "so that other girls will have the same chance I had." And she wants to share her surplus with a friend who is pregnant. "Now I understand," she said, "why everyone has given me so much. Giving really makes you happy!"

Frank: When Michele decided she wanted to keep the baby and not give it up for adoption, Dan and I thought about how we could help her and her baby without separating them. It was obvious that Michele and the baby would need the support of a family to help them deal with all the demands of life that would come their way. Dan and I also knew that there would have to be some policy changes in how government and foster care agencies have traditionally dealt with pregnant juvenile delinquents. County Probation Departments pay the cost of foster care placement for juvenile delinquents hoping that they will be rehabilitated. Probation Departments would have no obligation to pay the cost of rearing the baby because the baby would not have committed any offense.

Another problem was that foster care agencies, like the one I work with, have never permitted a pregnant teenager to keep her baby and remain in foster care. The agencies would encourage the teenager to have an abortion or give her baby up for adoption. If the young woman could somehow win a legal battle to keep her child, she and her child would be dismissed from foster care to fend for themselves. This usually meant that they would try to survive alone on public assistance—without the support of a family.

I was able to locate families willing to provide foster care for both Michele and her baby. Once I could prove to my director that there were families willing to rear both a teenager and her child, he gave us the go ahead to begin providing these services as long as we could obtain funding.

We were able to convince Michele's probation officer that Michele could care for her own baby with the help of a foster family, and even continue her education. The probation department agreed to continue financially supporting Michele while she and her baby were in foster care. We were also able to receive funds through the department of public assistance for her baby.

Michele and her son were the first mother and baby to be allowed to remain together while receiving the support of a foster family. Four months later, a young mother named Rachel and her daughter were able to begin the same type of foster care together. Furthermore, our agency had made plans to extend our foster care services to a greater number of women in Michele and Rachel's situation. It appears that permanent family-oriented policy changes have been the result of my boss and I working together for the same goal.

F. and E. S.

"The more we enter into the heart of our neighbor to share his or her sufferings and joys, the more our soul rises to union with God" (24).

The next two experiences show families reaching out to make themselves one with their neighbors. As a result, both they and these neighbors find themselves in closer union not only with one another, but also with God.

Block Party

Pete: In the neighborhood where we live it is an annual tradition to have a block party. We see this as a way to bring more unity within the block. We have a great variety of neighbors, from retired people in their eighties all the way down to young people in their twenties who are not married yet.

For the past twelve years or so we've taken it upon ourselves to help get this block party started. We tried to never have the attitude: "Well you did your time one year, now let somebody else try it." And we noticed that it was important not to back away from our accepted responsibility but to always be the first to love, not hoping that somebody else would do it. In this way we have developed not just as neighbors but as a kind of a family.

Iris: As can be expected, people have many ideas which can add variety to planning things like block parties, but may also lead to controversies. We have one neighbor, Ms. Jones, who has very strong ideas and even when most of the other people would not agree or would think that something else is better, she insists upon doing things her way. In fact one year she had a disc jockey come and play music. The music was so deafening that by eight o'clock everybody had left the street because it was no longer possible to converse.

The following year we decided to hire a renowned square dance caller to come and do a family square dance.

69

Since she had wanted to repeat the prior year's musical program, and the square dance was not what she had suggested, she just made other plans for herself that night, but left her children behind with a baby-sitter for the party.

As it turned out the square dance was a tremendous success. There were grandparents dancing with other people's two- and three-year-old grandchildren; the children of the neighborhood were ecstatic and had a wonderful time; everyone participated and no one was left out. Several families who were not able to be there had simply left their children with us, and therefore we tried to provide more food and care for them. This particular experience was a real effort to love in spite of suffering and division, trying to help everyone work together.

In the end everyone was very happy and pleased with the block party and talking about how wonderful it had been. When Ms. Jones heard all this, she came to thank us for the great joy that it had been for so many.

The following year when we were working on the block party Ms. Jones came once again with an idea that few agreed upon. In fact when we voted, her idea wasn't accepted. This time though she pitched in just the same and did it the way everyone else wanted to do it, giving her full support.

Over the years we have entertained ourselves in a variety of ways. There are now even family talent shows for everyone on the block.

Pete: Oftentimes I realize God has provided fruits as a result of trying to do everything out of love for the others. It so happened that last summer our car died and we temporarily needed another one. Ms. Jones happened to have a spare one. I can still remember asking to borrow it; she was quite happy to let us use it. It ended up that she let us use it for two weeks and at the end of the period when we returned the car we asked if we could give her something besides the gas which we had put in the car. She said, "No, you can't give me any money. I know you'd do the same for me." We realized that she understood something about how we try to do things.

Ms. Jones lives across the street, while on our side there are retired couples on both sides of us. On the right it's a husband and wife who are both semi-invalids. Some neighbors have rejected them for a variety of reasons. They are people who are somewhat hard to approach. They don't keep up their property very well and can be intimidating. On the left of us there's a man who actually helped build the houses in the neighborhood years ago. He keeps his distance perhaps because he doesn't feel comfortable around others. As a family we've tried to particularly reach out to these neighbors.

Iris: Many neighbors have tried to help the couple who live to the right of us but by the very circumstances it's very difficult and besides the house and yard are in very bad shape. Their behavior repulsed some neighbors and they tended to take advantage of neighbors who did help.

We assisted them in properly applying for social services so that they would be sure to receive the appropriate type. We also tried to help them solve the rodent and garbage problem in their home. Some neighbors renewed their efforts to care for these people, and helped us.

We have seen how trying to be a family really rooted in God, that tries to love, continually overlooking initial appearances and that focuses on seeing Jesus even in these neighbors helped other people renew their outlook toward them as well. Now our son, who is nine years old, goes regularly to visit the couple, and, through all the disarray, through all the difficult moments, helps them, waits on them, does whatever he's asked to do in order to be of service.

P. and I. F.

An Anniversary Party and the Man Whom Love Made King

Tony: There are many families around us, and in our daily routine of life we have had many encounters which have shown us that people long for something more than material possessions—in other words, for God.

Over the years, we have taken advantage of birthdays, illnesses, weddings, as well as Christmas and Easter holidays as opportunities to do acts of love for other people, and in so doing to bring peace and joy to the lives of many.

One of these occasions was our twenty-fifth wedding anniversary. We originally wanted to let it pass unnoticed thinking of the work and expense such a celebration would imply. However, our four sons decided they wanted to honor us with a big anniversary party.

Christine and I agreed out of love for them, thinking also that we could take the opportunity to invite many of our friends and neighbors, making it a celebration for everyone. While planning, we thought of a couple we had met on our honeymoon, but hadn't seen for fourteen years. They were married the same day and hour as ourselves. We decided to invite them to renew their marriage vows with us and have them share in the excitement and fun. They had no special plans for their anniversary and were delighted to accept the invitation.

Christine: When I called to tell them that our plans for the celebration included the Catholic Mass, there was a moment of silence on the other end. They explained to me that both they and their five daughters had been away from the Catholic Church for many years. I understood that the moment of the eucharist would be very difficult for all of them. What could be done? I bravely suggested that they go to confession with us, but the silence grew deeper and we said goodbye. Two days later the husband called to thank me for suggesting confession; they had all gone and were full of joy. They also accepted our invitation and would participate in our anniversary festivities. This was just the beginning of a series of small, but real miracles that the grace of God brought about through our anniversary.

Others followed. For example a friend of ours told us that while we were renewing our vows he understood that we had God present among us in our marriage, and realized in that moment that God was missing from his life. After twelve years he returned to church and has been faithful ever since.

A couple we had not seen in some years couldn't believe the change in us. When they realized that God has the first place in our life they felt the desire to come back to him after twenty years of being far away.

Many of our neighbors are non-practicing Catholics. Later they told us that they had come back to the sacraments in order to participate fully in the celebration of the Mass. Our own four boys did the same and this was the most beautiful gift for us that day.

The priest who celebrated the eucharist met quite a few of our friends, many of whom afterwards made appointments to see him. He told us that he felt that his sacrament of priesthood had been renewed by the love that our sacrament was giving to others in a marriage that had become a channel of the love of God for many.

Tony: The only place a reception for 130 people could be held was in our garden, but that morning the sky was very gray and rain was predicted. We couldn't afford to rent a tent and so all we could do was pray. However, a tent, tables, chairs and everything else that was needed arrived through an unknown friend who had heard of our situation and decided then and there to give us this surprise. He stayed for the party and at the end thanked us for having "brought such joy into his lonely life."

Christine: These are just a few moments of our life; there would be many other stories to tell. There is the story of a dear friend who had a painful experience during her illness. She went from indifference toward God and hostility toward us, to being united to God, though still suffering, and dying with him. She died surrounded by her family and ours.

One story that particularly touched us, however, is that of Sharon and Phil. They were extremely poor when we met them and were living on the brink of the abyss of drugs and alcohol. Their children were fearful and disorientated.

I remember Sharon's decision to give up drinking and taking drugs after a meeting of families in our home and Phil's anger at this and his attempts to dissuade her. She was determined and persevered. One night she managed to bring Phil to our house and, although he vented his atheistic, hopeless feelings on us, love gradually won him over until he began to feel at ease with us.

From then on their story became ours. We were overjoyed when Phil gave up drugs, and a friend of ours offered him a job. And when the families around us helped them find a decent home, furniture and clothes for the whole family they began to discover through God's providence in their life the love of a Father who takes care of everything. And when Sharon decided to come back to the church after seventeen years, Phil shared her joy. He told us, "After all that I have experienced, how can I not believe in God? I feel like a king!"

His brief story ended here. A car accident took his life shortly after. Both we and Sharon remember him just like that: a man whom love had made a king. Sharon is still close to us. "That which you have given me," she tells us, "has an always deeper meaning."

T. and C. M.

> *"The laity . . . find their way to God right there in the midst of the world, where they live shoulder to shoulder with neighbors of every kind" (23).*
>
> *These last four examples show how families centered in prayer turn towards those who have been placed in their paths, especially other families threatened with dissolution. They illustrate in their experience an example of mutual prayer.*

A Family Reunited

As a school teacher I have a lot of contacts with families through their children. So many of them have problems that would simply overwhelm me at times.

A short time ago I had a student in my class whose mother was dying of a terminal illness. The disease was progressing very slowly, taking a small part of this woman at a time. To make matters worse, her husband was unable to cope with the problem and left the family. Slowly but surely this mother of three children became less and less physically capable of caring for her family. The children took on more and more responsibility and although it was extremely difficult for them, the family was managing.

One day a lady from the child protection agency came to my classroom and took the daughter away. I found out later that they had removed her from home and separated her from her brothers by sending each of them to different foster homes. The counselor informed me that the home was unfit for the children to live in and they would not be permitted to return to the mother until the place had been cleaned up. It happened that a relative of the family was visiting who later called to tell me of the problem in detail. I asked him to come to school where we could sit and talk in depth about what had happened and what could be done.

During that meeting I listened intensely to what he said. I knew the only thing that mattered was to love and that meant listening. He explained that the house needed some work but there wasn't enough money to do it. I asked if I could help in any way. He didn't know how but he said he would be open to whatever I could do. I went home and prayed that everyone involved would be able to find God's love in this, believing that it is true that, no matter what, God loves us immensely.

I shared this with my wife Joan and told her of my desire that we be united in Christ so that he, among us, could help us find a way to help. We talked about it for a while and decided to make some calls to other families. Within a very short time food, clothing, and money was being delivered to our door. The next day I delivered the items to the mother. She was very happy and she opened her heart to me and told me of her frustration and her desire to be with her children.

During the summer I regularly do light jobs to earn some extra money. I asked her if I could look around the house to see if there was anything I could do. A lot of work needed to be done but the most striking thing was this poor woman's bed. The mattress was completely worn out. It was causing her much discomfort and loss of sleep.

The following day I explained the whole situation to the other teachers in my building. One teacher donated enough money to buy a new mattress and box spring. Others said they would ask their husbands if they would be willing to help fix up the house. Still others donated money. After only three days, enough money was collected to buy all of the paint, plaster, and other materials to do all of the work. Ten men and two women went to the house that very weekend. They completely painted the interior of the home, and replaced the ceiling that had been damaged due to a roof leak. In all, the house was beautiful and the children could come back home.

To see the look on the faces of the children and the mother when they were reunited was nothing short of beautiful. I went home that day with praise to God on my lips and in my heart for all that happened. After that day many other families became involved helping to care for the children and the house.

J. M.

The Results of a Casual Stroll

Several years ago, as I was taking a walk with my children in the neighborhood, I met a young mother. There were children playing in her yard and she was just sitting there looking very tired and not too happy. She was pregnant and the look on her face prompted me to go over and greet her. I introduced myself and we began to talk. She shared things with me about her life, her marriage and the struggles she was having. I was struck with her immediate trust in me. It was obvious that she was not happy, especially in this pregnancy and I tried to make her unhappiness mine and listen.

One of her concerns was for baby clothes; she had none. I told her I would look through my things at home and share whatever I had. She was moved by this gesture, and very happy for the visit and generosity. A few days later I went back to her home and gave her enough baby clothing to get her started along with a gift of diapers and other little necessary items. That began my relationship with my neighbor that would take me through her many sufferings over the years.

After the birth of her baby, I took the opportunity to have her and her children over for an afternoon of swimming and play that gave us a chance to be together. She was going through a rough time in her marriage for various reasons, one of which was financial. Her husband couldn't seem to keep a job, so they were living from week to week never knowing if they would have the money to buy groceries.

Whatever extra I had, I shared with her and after telling my friends who were also living the gospel with me, we were able to meet many of her urgent needs. She began to

77

feel stronger because of the many people who were helping her. I made it a point to spend as much time with her as possible. I baby-sat her children so that she could spend time with her husband and eventually we began to talk about God. Her husband was never friendly and seldom spoke. Many times I felt uneasy but knew his struggles and tried to be of service whenever possible.

The next two years were ones with many sufferings and once she even thought of leaving him. I could sense her pain, but I knew that leaving wasn't the answer. I suggested that we try to live a phrase from scripture and I told her that God would give her the strength to face each new situation. It wouldn't be easy but she decided to try it. It gave her new hope and determination and for a while things looked better.

Then one day she called telling me she was pregnant again and, considering everything in her life, was going to abort the baby as soon as possible. She also informed me that when she shared the news of the pregnancy with her husband he became angry and took his frustrations out on her. She feared for her life and I knew her call to me was a cry for help. I immediately went over to her house and took her and the children out to dinner so that we could talk. I offered my home, but it obviously would be the first place her husband would look, so we found an interim place for a few days.

During those days we prayed for light and understanding and I prayed that this new life would be spared and she and her husband would be reconciled. After some time, she was back at home and although things weren't perfect a certain calmness had returned. Deep down I didn't think she wanted to go through with an abortion, it just seemed the easiest solution to her.

We did a lot of talking over the next two weeks and I asked my friends to also pray that she would make the right decision. I assured her she was not alone and that I would be there to help her in every way except to terminate the pregnancy. Waiting those days was an agony that I will never forget. I deeply discovered what it means to suffer with those who suffer.

Finally one day she called me to tell me that she and her husband had done a lot of talking and realized that neither one of them could go through an abortion. It was close to Christmas at the time, and I felt that in that moment we had received the greatest Christmas gift of all. I sent her flowers and called her back to see if I could do anything for her. She explained to me that she and her husband had delayed their Christmas shopping because of all that had happened and they needed a hand toy shopping for the children. When I arrived, I was greeted very warmly and her husband even embraced me. As we were leaving the house to go, she whispered in my ear that the money they were going to use for the abortion was going to be spent on toys for the children.

Our lives continued, and even though she and her family moved a couple of times we always remained in touch. Once, over the holidays they were in need of a food basket, toys and other things; friends of mine were able to provide everything. The lady I used to baby-sit for even gave me one hundred dollars for them to use for family bills. The following Christmas this same lady called to tell me that she had some left over boxes of food and toys from a Christmas toy drive and felt I could share them with my former neighbor and her family. There were so many gifts that we were able to share them not only with her family but with several other families besides. Eventually my home became the repository for all kinds of goods. Whenever there was a need, God always provided exactly what was needed.

My friend could readily see God's love for her because gradually, this life of sharing became hers too. She would call me to tell me that she gave a sweater to a neighbor who needed one and would be so happy inside to be able to do such acts of love. And when I told her that someone needed a crib for their baby, she went out and looked until she found one that they could use.

The rapport and love that has been strengthened over

the years with this family is very beautiful. She has since had her children baptized and sees that they all make it to weekly services. Also her husband readily shares with me now and each time I see their youngest child, I remember that God's love is stronger than anything else and that with it, we can overcome every obstacle.

T. L.

In Place of T.V.

I never really watched a lot of T.V. in the past, but enjoyed seeing the news over and over during the day as well as some of the talk shows. I would refer to them as being educational and would feel comfortable with them on while I was working around the house.

One day I was studying together with some others the harms that T.V. often brings into our homes and within ourselves. We decided to make an effort to leave the T.V. off and concentrate on all the other things that its use has pushed out of our life, especially our relationship with God and the people around us.

I went to Mass the next morning and prayed for help to have the willpower to not turn on my T.V. that day. I felt I needed to take it a day at a time. I kept it off. At one point I asked Jesus to talk to me and tell me anything he wanted me to know as I was now quietly listening without outside distractions. It came to mind to call a young wife and mother, the sister-in-law of a friend of mine who lives very far away. This friend had asked me to check up on her brother and sister-in-law and their sixteen-month-old girl. They had moved some years ago to Springville and she was worried about them. Though they had been married in the Catholic Church over three years ago, they had not been back since and did not have their little girl baptized. They were both using drugs and her brother was also drinking heavily.

When I first heard of this situation months ago, I invited Cathy, the sister-in-law, to a young mothers meeting I had formed in the Springville area where several young mothers and myself would meet and read the Word of Life, a commentary to a phrase from scripture, and talk about our lives and goals always focusing on the gospel. Cathy and her little girl, Stacy, came one time last fall and never came back although I would call her each month. I did not know how serious their situation was.

In this moment I felt urged to call her. It was a little clumsy because I did not know her well at all. I called and as we talked I sensed she was really troubled. I asked her if she was free the next day to have coffee with me. She readily said yes and invited me to her home. Her home was neat but like a smoke den. She said nothing was done in the house because all her husband did on his time off was drink and smoke pot; he was high most of the time. She told me she would get so discouraged that often she would join him in "escaping" too.

I asked her if she was worried about little Stacy. She said yes and in fact just that night before I called, had thought seriously of leaving her husband. She couldn't take any more. I kept asking Jesus to help me be a good listener and inspire me in what I would say. I knew he was guiding me as we spoke.

I asked her what I could do. Had she turned to God through all this? I told her I knew she and Danny were born and raised in Catholic homes. She said she was feeling guilty that Stacy was so old and still not baptized. She had asked the priest who married them if he would baptize her but he told her, because they were not practicing their faith, he could not. When I asked her if she understood this, she said yes. I then asked her if she would like to come back to the sacraments and have Stacy baptized. I would walk the distance with her and help her in any way she needed. She asked if I would talk to our pastor and see if he would meet with her. I agreed to immediately do so. When I left she was smiling. She said she was already feeling at peace and was happy. She spoke no more that afternoon of leaving her husband.

I called Cathy's pastor and he was very happy to hear what I had to say. He wanted Cathy to take the next step and personally call him to set up a time. She did and I baby-sat the day she went to see him.

I felt I had to take all this a step further and introduce her to my friends. She had told me that all of hers get high so it was obvious that she would need a new circle of friends. While she was at her meeting with the pastor, I invited another young mother and her little son over for coffee so they would be there when Cathy came back. My friend offered her friendship and baby-sitting services. She also spoke about activities in the parish which involved other young mothers. We all thought this could help her make new friends. Cathy was very happy.

Things with the pastor went well. She said, with tears in her eyes, that Stacy could be baptized and even though Danny would not go to church with her she wanted to begin to go every Sunday and involve herself together with Stacy. She gave us the date of the baptism and invited all of us. We told her we'd have a real celebration. She was so happy that day and even agreed that she would stay with Danny and take him to church in her heart until the day that he too was ready to change.

My husband Mark and I pick Cathy up for Mass on Sundays and we will continue to do so until she feels comfortable going alone.

I am constantly in awe of the power of living this life of working for unity. If I would have had the T.V. on that morning, I would have missed the inspiration of the Holy Spirit to make that call. I see how God's work can only be completed by us if we are available. I know for sure that I cannot serve two masters at the same time.

D. W.

There is Always Something That Can Be Done

Leroy: One day last fall, as I walked to my car after work, I saw a woman and child approaching people in the parking lot. The woman was asking for money. As I got closer I could see they were very poor. Their clothes were dirty and worn.

She asked for money, saying they had recently moved from another city and her husband was unable to find work. As a consequence, they were living on the streets. As we spoke, her husband appeared with another child in tow. (The boy was four, their little girl, five.)

Since I work in the downtown district of a large city, I often see people who live on the streets and ask for money. Each time I am reminded of Jesus' description of the last judgment, "I was hungry and you gave me to eat." This time, I was particularly pained by the fact that not only these adults, but also their children were living on the streets.

I asked them if they had gone to any of the churches in the area for help. They said they had but were unable to get assistance.

I only had a one dollar bill in my wallet. I could see the anguish in their faces. I told them I left work about the same time every day; perhaps they could come back.

On the way home I could not get this little, helpless family off my mind.

Ann: I was cooking dinner when Leroy came in and told me about this family. We just couldn't think of sitting down to dinner knowing they might not have anything. We put together some food and went back downtown to look for them. They were nowhere to be found. We just hoped and prayed they were all right.

Leroy: The next day when I got to my car, they were there. They had found a place to stay for a week for a certain amount, which I gave them. I also gave them the food, which I had kept in the car.

I stayed to talk and find out more about them and their

situation. We had a lot of clothes for adults and children at home, all donated by various families, friends of ours. I felt it was important for me to call them by their first names, and Henry and Beth did the same with me.

Every couple of days I would find them waiting for me at my car. I began keeping clothes and food there on a regular basis in the event they would show up. They were always very thankful, and I felt they were sincere.

They told me on a number of occasions that though they had asked many, we were the only ones interested in them. Whenever I gave them something, I told them that we were not the only ones helping, but there were several other families who cared about them and had contributed.

Life for them in a new city was difficult for the next couple of months. Off and on they and the children were back living in the streets. Henry would get a temporary job, and they would have a place to stay. Then the job would end, money would run out and they would have to move on.

We couldn't abandon them. We didn't know their history, but it seemed they'd been living this nomadic sort of life for quite a while. Henry had little formal education and never had a job to make enough to support four people. Beth took care of the kids and sometimes found odd jobs if he wasn't working.

After several months, through their own efforts, Henry and Beth applied and qualified for government-assisted housing. Their troubles continued, though, since Henry was still unable to find steady work. Then he suddenly had to leave to care for his mother who was terminally ill in another city. That was about a month before Christmas.

Ann: Leroy and I and our boys continued to go by their apartment, bringing Beth and the children food, clothing, blankets and other things they needed.

We learned how important it is to be open to the needs of other families as a way of fostering unity in the world around us. We didn't want Henry and Beth to know only us; we wanted to share the experience so it could be a gift for other families, too. They were eager to help.

There were about ten families and many other friends and co-workers doing what they could to fill the gap for this needy family. That's what we do for each other.

As Christmas got closer, we invited them to a Christmas party for families. Henry was still out of town, but Beth and the children came. We tried to focus on the true meaning of Christmas. This was the closest we had come to talking about God in any way. It was a time for family, and they seemed to enjoy it.

I asked Beth about her own family. She said she had a disagreement with her mother, and that was why they had moved here. She didn't say what had happened but it must have been serious.

Something changed for Beth. Just before Christmas she called her mother, and invited her to come and visit for a few days. She was very happy.

Leroy: We put together food, presents and clothing which a number of families had given us for them. On Christmas Eve I brought the things to them. Henry was still out of town with his mother, who died several weeks later.

Beth and the children were frightened because their apartment had been broken into and the thief had not been caught. Beth assured me, however, she and the kids would be fine. They thanked us for the food and gifts and wished us a Merry Christmas.

That evening at home our family celebrated Christmas Eve by having two of my brothers from out of town over for dinner. We stayed up late preparing our gifts. We finished after midnight and, exhausted from the day, we were just getting ready to go to sleep when the phone rang.

It was Beth. Someone had tried to break in. She asked if she and her children could come to spend the night with us.

Our house was full, but we couldn't leave this family in such a situation. We decided to put them up in a motel.

At 2:00 A.M. Christmas morning we picked up this young mother and her two children in a pretty rough part of town and then drove around looking for a place for them to stay. Later, in reflecting on this scene, we thought of Joseph and

Mary looking for a place to stay. In fact, when we stopped at the first motel, the office door was locked. After I continued to knock, someone inside made a small opening in the door and asked what we wanted. I explained that we were trying to find a place for a frightened family to stay, but that I had no cash. Through the crack in the door, the person inside replied that they took only cash and promptly locked the door. We went on until we finally found a place.

Ann: We arranged for them to stay at the motel also Christmas night, so they could at least enjoy a peaceful Christmas without fear. That evening, Beth called. She had gone back to the apartment to get medicine and clothes for the kids and found that her mother had arrived a day early. They missed the last bus for the day that could take them back to the motel and they had no way to get back.

"I'll go this time," I told Leroy. Our eighteen-year-old son Bill went with me. As we drove I felt the need to explain, "Sometimes the things your father and I do, the situations we get ourselves into, may be hard for you to understand. But I hope you can see that helping this family to the very end is something we want to do for God." Bill's reply really came from the heart: "Maybe I'm not ready for what you're doing, but I believe in it."

When we reached the apartment, we packed everyone in the car and helped them get warm. The grandmother whom we'd never met before, thanked us and told me many things about herself and her daughter and the whole family situation—things you wouldn't tell a stranger.

It was beautiful to see the mother and daughter together again at Christmas. That night as we left, Beth said to me, "Pray for us." And I assured her, "We do."

Leroy: Our Christmas turned out quite differently from what we had planned, but it left us feeling closer to the real meaning of Christmas.

Since then, Beth has expressed her desire to live differently, to "turn her life over to the Lord," as she said. Since we had been treating her and her family in a Christian way, she understood she needed to do the same.

86

We were able to even find a job for Henry. The story continues.

A. and L. P.

Also available in the same series:

THE FAMILY AND EDUCATION
Teaching as Jesus Did
John Olsen, CFX and T. Masters (eds.)

"Both parents and children profit when parents undertake seriously the religious formation of their children, as the U.S. Bishops pointed out. This book is a compilation of experiences of parents in the form of short vignettes to illustrate this. The different slices of real life detailed in this book will be as points of light to many others faced with similar difficulties and encouragement to them in their commitment to Christ and to one another. Another valuable resource for the Catholic family trying to be fully Christian." *Liguorian*

    Series: Family Life—ISBN 0-911782-73-7, paper, 112 pp.

THE FAMILY—A COMMUNITY OF LOVE
by Igino Giordani

What is the true nature and purpose of the family? From where does it derive the strength, stability, and warmth of love that makes it the foundation of the life of society itself? *The Family-A Community of Love* "was originally written in 1969 by one of Italy's foremost religious authors, in response to the new horizons on the family opened up by the Second Vatican Council; Giordani describes the place of the family in the church and the world." *Spiritual Life*

    Series: Family Life—ISBN 0-911782-71-0, paper, 96 pp.

SEX REDEEMED
by Michel Pochet

Sex Redeemed is not just another book about sex. It presents a depth of understanding and a range of insights that can hardly fail to fascinate and be helpful to many people, particularly the young. It was written after years of intimate conversations with married, engaged, and single people, which is perhaps one reason for its qualities: sensitivity, openness, warmth, the awareness of human dignity. *Sex Redeemed* is an excellent guide for all those parents, pastors or teachers who are looking for a clearer understanding of sexuality with particular reference to the young.

    Series: Family Life—ISBN 0-904287-31-9, paper, 64 pp.